How to Pray the Secret Rosary

~~~

by Frank M. Rega, OFS

Copyright © 2016 Frank M. Rega

All rights reserved.

ISBN-10: 1530074290
ISBN-13: 978-1530074297

DEDICATION

This book is dedicated to you the reader.

You are encouraged to write in this book!

This book is designed for your use.

Space is provided for your personal meditations and notes.

This book belongs to:

_____

Contents

i	Overview	1
ii	Genesis of This Work	3
iii	The Four Mini-Gospels	7
1	First "Ave" – Humility	13
2	Second "Ave" – Meekness	21
3	Third "Ave" – Sorrow for Sin	27
4	Fourth "Ave" – Faith	33
5	Fifth "Ave" – Hope	41
6	Sixth "Ave" – Love	47
7	Seventh "Ave" – Abandonment	55
8	Eighth "Ave" – The Father	61
9	Ninth "Ave" – The Son	69
10	Tenth "Ave" – The Holy Spirit	79

11	Praying the Traditional Rosary	89
12	More on Humility	99
13	Fatima and the Rosary	105
14	Padre Pio and The Rosary	109
15	How many Rosaries Should One Pray?	117
	Bibliography	119

About the cover image:

The image of a rainbow rose is courtesy of Themes.com, a web site of wallpapers and backgrounds that can be used by the public.
      http://7-themes.com/7000040-rainbow-flowers.html

How to Pray the Secret Rosary

i. Overview

This work is intended for those who already pray the Rosary as well as for those who wish to learn to pray it. For the latter, who may be unfamiliar with the prayers, mysteries, and history of the Rosary, these are set out in Chapter 11. The reader should have an understanding of the basic concept of the decade of ten "Hail Mary" prayers that are the back-bone of each of the sacred mysteries in the lives of Jesus and Mary, upon which the Rosary is based. This decade of "Hail Mary" prayers, or angelic salutations, comprises chapters numbered one through ten.

Each of the ten "Hail Mary" prayers has a key idea or concept attached to it. The first seven prayers are keyed to one of the seven pillars of wisdom. The seven pillars are derived from the four scriptural "mini-gospels," described below in chapter iii. The last three "Hail Marys" are associated in turn with the Father, the Son, and the Holy Spirit.

For instance, for the first mystery of the Holy Rosary, the Annunciation, there are ten Hail Marys to be prayed. Each of these ten prayers has a fixed concept or key idea attached to it. For the first Hail Mary, the concept is "humility," for the second it is 'meekness' and so on. When it is time to pray the second mystery of the Rosary, the Visitation, the decade of angelic salutations is revisited, beginning again with the idea of "humility" for the first Hail Mary.

Memorizing the idea or concept associated with each of the ten angelic salutations brings greater spiritual depth to praying the Rosary. Furthermore, it has the added benefit of allowing one to pray the Rosary in situations where no beads are available, and without the need for actually counting ten "Hail Marys."

It is not far-fetched to conceive of a time, even in the United States, where the a so-called separation of Church and state might reach such a point that public display of one's religion may be forbidden. It had already occurred in Ireland during the penal times, which led to the Rosary being prayed inconspicuously, using a small "finger Rosary" with a ring of ten beads. If the need should ever arise again to pray an outlawed Rosary in complete secrecy, one can have recourse to the method of praying the "*Secret Rosary*" contained herein.

♦♦♦

ii. Genesis of this Work

This short treatise is the outcome of over 30 years of preparation. I began collecting passages and writing my thoughts and meditations on the various aspects of Catholic spirituality in the early 1980's, compiling them in a loose-leaf notebook. I cannot recall for certain what inspired that effort, but I believe it sprang from reading an exceptional spiritual book called *Humility of Heart*, by Fr. Cajetan Mary da Bergamo, published by TAN Books. This work emphasizes the vital importance of humility as the necessary foundation for the growth of the soul's spiritual life. I was so impressed by it that I started to write out the passages that seemed to me to be critical for my own spiritual progress.

Soon afterwards, probably in the mid-1980's, I began to read and meditate on Fr. Peter J. Arnoudt's magnificent treatise on the spiritual life, *The Imitation of the Sacred Heart of Jesus* (TAN Books). The very first line in the first chapter quotes these words of our Lord: "Learn of me because I am meek and humble of heart: and ye shall find rest for your souls." (Mt 11: 29.) I am on my third copy of this book, the first two having been read and underlined so frequently that the pages seem to have melted. But this first line, which the author terms the foundation of the entire book, recalls to mind a similar teaching of the Lord on humility and meekness: the beatitudes.

The first two beatitudes from the fifth chapter of the Gospel of St. Matthew are "blessed are the poor in spirit," and "blessed are the meek," that is, humility and meekness. The subsequent five beatitudes refer to mourning, justice, mercy, purity and peace. Thus when the Lord said in Matthew 11:29, "Learn of me because I am meek and humble of heart," it is as if he were implying the rest of the beatitudes were to follow. "Learn of me because I am meek and humble, I mourn for sin, I am just, merciful, pure of heart, and a peacemaker."

Wisdom hath built herself a house, she hath hewn her out seven pillars (Prov. 9: 1)

As I began to take notes on these seven beatitudes, I learned that St. Thomas Aquinas correlated them to the seven gifts of the Holy Spirit, as given in Isaiah 11:2-3. For example, the beatitude "blessed are the poor in spirit" corresponds to the gift of "fear of the Lord." (*Summa,* II-II, Q 19, a. 12.) (The seven gifts are listed in the below chapter on the Four Mini-Gospels.)

Eventually, I became curious about two other "sevens," the seven petitions of the Lord's Prayer, and the seven last words of Jesus on the cross, and sought a correlation between these four groups of "sevens." I found a confirmation of my attempt in the works of St. Augustine, who established a correspondence with each of the petitions of the Lord's Prayer to the Beatitudes and to the Gifts of the Holy Spirit (*Sermon on the*

Mount, Newman Press, pp. 125-127). Then relatively recently, I discovered that Bishop Fulton J. Sheen had made an effort to tie the seven last words on the cross with the beatitudes (*The Cross and the Beatitudes*, Liguori/Triumph).

The connection among the four mini-gospels to each other along each of the seven steps or pillars of wisdom is usually obvious, but not in all cases. Sometimes one has to exercise the faculty of meditation to see the relationship.

In sum, there are seven pillars of spirituality or of wisdom, given in four separate locations in Scripture. Let us see how the seven pillars tie in with the Rosary and the decade of ten Hail Marys or Aves that are prayed with each mystery. At some point, I decided to match each one of the seven pillars with each of the first seven "Hail Mary" prayers that are part of a decade of the Rosary. What about the last three Aves? The obvious association for the last three "Hail Marys" is to the Blessed Trinity – Father, Son and Holy Spirit.

The connection of each Hail Mary with its appropriate concept is surprisingly easy to memorize. The first Ave is the first of the pillars of wisdom, which is humility. The second is meekness, the third is sorrow for sin, followed by faith, hope, love, and the seventh is abandonment. The last three of course are the three persons of the Holy Trinity. The advantage of this association of the "seven pillars" and the Trinity with the ten Hail Marys or Ave's soon becomes evident: if necessary, one can pray this "*Secret Rosary*" without any beads at all. Whenever I am not able to use my beads while praying (such as doing chores, shaving, or in the shower) I can still pray an entire decade of the Rosary by recalling the spiritual concept associated with each Ave. Nor is there a need to count from one to ten on one's fingers in order to keep track of the Hail Marys that are prayed!

But what about the eighth beatitude?

The gospel of St. Matthew actually lists eight beatitudes, culminating in: "Blessed are they that suffer persecution for justice' sake: for theirs is the kingdom of heaven." (Mt. 5: 10.) However, most commentators are in agreement with St. Thomas Aquinas, who considered the proper enumeration of the beatitudes to be seven:

"The eighth beatitude is a confirmation and declaration of all those that precede. Because from the very fact that a man is confirmed in poverty of spirit, meekness, and the rest, it follows that no persecution will induce him to renounce them. Hence the eighth beatitude corresponds, in a way, to all the preceding seven." (*Summa*, I-II, Q. 69, a.3.)

♦♦♦

How to Pray the Secret Rosary

iii. The Four Mini-Gospels

The seven gifts of the Holy Spirit, the seven beatitudes, the seven petitions of the Lord's prayer, and the seven words on the cross comprise the four mini-gospels contained in scripture. Their correspondence with each other and their appellation as 'mini-gospels' was initially set forth in my blog post of September 2015: http://divinefiat.blogspot.com/2015/09/the-four-mini-gospels.html

The first seven Aves of each decade of the Rosary correspond to the seven pillars of Wisdom as delineated below:

I.

The Seven Gifts of the Holy Spirit: (Is. 11:2,3).

1. Fear of the Lord
2. Piety
3. Knowledge
4. Fortitude
5. Counsel
6. Understanding
7. Wisdom

II.

The Beatitudes: (Mt. 5: 3-9).

1. Blessed are the poor in spirit for theirs is the Kingdom of heaven.

2. Blessed are the meek for they shall possess the land.

3. Blessed are they that mourn for they shall be comforted.

4. Blessed are they that hunger and thirst after justice for they shall have their fill.

5. Blessed are the merciful for they shall obtain mercy.

6. Blessed are the clean of heart for they shall see God.

7. Blessed are the peacemakers for they shall be called children of God.

III.

The Lord's Prayer: (Mt. 6: 9-13; Lk. 11: 2-4).

1. Our Father who art in heaven hallowed by thy name.

2. Thy kingdom come.

3. Thy will be done on earth as it is in heaven.

4. Give us this day our daily bread.

5. And forgive us our trespasses as we forgive those who trespass against us.

6. And lead us not into temptation,

7. But deliver us from evil.

IV.

The Seven Words on the Cross:

1. "Father, forgive them for they know not what they do." (Lk. 23:34.)

2. "Amen, I say to thee: this day thou shalt be with me in paradise." (Lk. 23:43.)

3. "Woman, behold thy son." To the disciple, "Behold your mother." (Jn. 19:26-27.)

4. "My God, my God, why hast thou forsaken me?" (Mk. 15:34.)

5. "I thirst." (Jn. 19:28.)

6. "It is consummated." (Jn. 19:30.)

7. "Father, into thy hands I commend my spirit." (Lk. 23:46.)

How to Pray the Secret Rosary

These seven pillars of wisdom can be set forth the following way, showing the four mini-gospel sources for each pillar. The next ten chapters expand on this summary table, relating the pillars to the first seven Hail Marys in a decade of the Rosary, with the last three Aves devoted to the Father, Son and Holy Spirit.

First Pillar: Key concept: Humility.

- *Gift*: Fear of the Lord.
- *Beatitude:* Blessed are the poor in spirit for theirs is the Kingdom of heaven.
- *Lord's Prayer:* Our Father who art in heaven hallowed by thy name.
- *Word on the Cross*: "Father, forgive them for they know not what they do."

~ ~ ~

Second Pillar: Key concept: Meekness.

- *Gift*: Piety.
- *Beatitude:* Blessed are the meek for they shall possess the land.
- *Lord's Prayer:* Thy kingdom come.
- *Word on the Cross*: "Amen, I say to thee: this day thou shalt be with me in paradise."

How to Pray the Secret Rosary

Third Pillar: Key concept: Sorrow for Sin.

° *Gift*: Knowledge.
° *Beatitude:* Blessed are they that mourn for they shall be comforted.
° *Lord's Prayer:* Thy will be done on earth as it is in heaven.
° *Word on the Cross*: "Woman, behold thy son." To the disciple, "Behold your mother."

~ ~ ~

Fourth Pillar: Key concept: Faith.

° *Gift*: Fortitude.
° *Beatitude:* Blessed are they that hunger and thirst after justice for they shall have their fill.
° *Lord's Prayer:* Give us this day our daily bread.
° *Word on the Cross*: "My God, my God, why hast thou forsaken me?"

~ ~ ~

Fifth Pillar: Key concept: Hope.

° *Gift*: Counsel.
° *Beatitude:* Blessed are the merciful for they shall obtain mercy.
° *Lord's Prayer:* And forgive us our trespasses as we forgive those who trespass against us.
° *Word on the Cross*: "I thirst."

Sixth Pillar: Key concept: Love.

○ *Gift*: Understanding.
○ *Beatitude:* Blessed are the clean of heart for they shall see God.
○ *Lord's Prayer:* And lead us not into temptation.
○ *Word on the Cross*: "It is consummated."

~ ~ ~

Seventh Pillar: Key concept: Abandonment.

○ *Gift*: Wisdom.
○ *Beatitude:* Blessed are the peacemakers for they shall be called children of God.
○ *Lord's Prayer:* But deliver us from evil.
○ *Word on the Cross*: "Father, into thy hands I commend my spirit."

♦♦♦

Chapter One

The First "Hail Mary"

Humility

Gift: Fear of the Lord.

Beatitude: Blessed are the poor in spirit for theirs is the kingdom of heaven.

Lord's Prayer: Our Father Who are in Heaven hallowed be Thy name.

Word on the Cross: "Father, forgive them for they know not what they do."

St. Augustine: "For if it is the fear of God through which the poor in spirit are blessed, inasmuch as theirs is the kingdom of heaven; let us ask that the name of God may be hallowed among men through that fear which is clean, enduring for ever." (*Sermon on the Mount*, Newman Press, pp. 125-127).

How to Pray the Secret Rosary

Considerations and Reflections

Fear of the Lord: This is filial fear, the fear of hurting or offending someone loved, as we realize our own weakness and vulnerability and sinfulness.

Fear of the Lord: reverence.

Poor in Spirit: The lowly, the humble, who are far from the spirit of pride, who do not covet the things of this world, whose spirit is raised to the things that concern heaven.

Hallowed be Thy name: Acknowledging the greatness of the Lord, we are humbled.

Perhaps the greatest reason for us to be humble, is that we are all members of that race, the human race, that crucified the Son of God.

The opposing vice to the virtue of humility is pride.

The poor in spirit vs. love of riches: "For the desire of money is the root of all evils; which some coveting have erred from the faith, and have entangled themselves in many sorrows (1 Tim. 6:10).

Poverty of our will in favor of the Lord's Will.

John the Baptist on the Lord: "He must increase, but I must decrease (Jn. 3:30).

"As St. Bernard remarks, this virtue [of poverty] does not consist only in being poor, but in loving poverty. Therefore did Jesus Christ say, 'Blessed are the poor in spirit, for theirs is the kingdom of heaven.' They are blessed because they desire nothing but God, and in God they find every good; in poverty they find their paradise on earth, as Saint Francis did when he exclaimed, 'My God and my all.'" (St. Alphonsus Liguori, *The Glories of Mary*, TAN Books, p. 492.)

"The fear of the Lord is the beginning of wisdom:" (Prov. 1:7; Prov. 9:10; Ps. 110(111):10; Ecclus. 1:16.)

Only when the soul realizes its nothingness before the Lord, and truly seeks the heavenly kingdom, does it begin to realize that the attainment of heaven is the only thing that matters – all earthly things are nothing. Heretofore the soul had acted as if it were crucifying the Lord, by being indifferent to heavenly inspirations, by rejecting grace – not understanding what it was doing. Now wisdom begins to dawn: the fear of the Lord is the beginning of wisdom. The soul comes to realize that God alone has the power to grant heaven to the soul.

Humility is one of the seven spirits of God:
"And this Holy Spirit is in Scripture especially spoken of by the number seven, whether in Isaiah or in the

Apocalypse, where the seven Spirits of God are most directly mentioned, on account of the sevenfold operation of one and the self-same Spirit (Rev. 1:20). And this sevenfold operation is mentioned in Isaiah (Is. 11:2). ...Hence also the Holy Spirit is spoken of under the number seven." (St. Augustine, *Exposition on Psalm 150*, www.newadvent.org/fathers).

True humility is doing the Will of God.

You, Oh Lord, are humility; in your humanity you became humility; in your knowledge from all eternity of your taking on human suffering in time, you were the spirit of humility.

Humility is truth. The seeking of the truth – searching for the truth – is the spirit of humility. If humility is truth, pride is the lie, since pride makes more of us than we really are in truth. Truth is born out of humility, just as The Truth was born out of the humility of the Blessed Virgin Mary. He who loves humility loves Jesus, since God is truth.

The Eucharist is the bread of humility.

Humility and confidence: "In the fear of the Lord is confidence of strength." (Prov. 14:26.)

Nothing is so fruitful on earth as true humility (Fr. Gabriel Palau, S.J., *The Active Catholic*, TAN Books, p. 111).

The more there shine forth in thee true humility, the greater will be the splendour of thy works (Fr. Gabriel Palau S.J., *ibid.,* p. 89).

"Jugis pax cum humili - Lasting peace is the lot of the humble." (St. Peter Julian Eymard, *The Real Presence,* p. 217).

Meditation on the self-abasement of Our Lord in the sacrament is the true road to humility (*Ibid.*, p. 201).

Humility is the pearl of great price. "Who when he had found one pearl of great price, went his way, and sold all that he had, and bought it." (Mt 13:46.)

Humility is the treasure hidden in a field. "The kingdom of heaven is like unto a treasure hidden in a field, which a man having found, hid it, and for joy goeth, and selleth all that he hath, and buyeth that field." (Mt. 13:44).

He that hath been humbled shall be in glory; and he that shall bow down his eyes, he shall be saved (Job 22:29).

Humility is the one thing necessary "Because God resisteth the proud and giveth grace to the humble." (Ja. 4:6); "For God resisteth the proud, but to the humble he giveth grace." (1 Peter 5:5.)

Humility is union with God, the foundation of all virtues, and the narrow way.

Humility goeth before glory (Prov. 15:33).

The prayer of him that humbleth himself shall pierce the clouds (Ecclus. 35:21).

He comforteth the humble (2 Cor. 7:6).

Where humility is, there also is wisdom (Prov. 11:2).

Because every one that exalteth himself, shall be humbled; and he that humbleth himself, shall be exalted (Lk. 14:11).

Let us try to be more and more humble, and if we obtain something it's given to us out of His infinite goodness (Padre Pio, *Padre Pio Teaches Us*, p. 106).

You must always be truthful my daughter. Humility is always truth (*Ibid.*, p. 105).

Please refer to Chapter 12 for more quotes and selections on the critical importance and absolute necessity of Humility.

♦♦♦

How to Pray the Secret Rosary

Personal reflections on humility:

How to Pray the Secret Rosary

Personal reflections on humility:

Chapter Two

The Second "Hail Mary"

Meekness

Gift: Piety.

Beatitude: Blessed are the meek for they shall possess the land.

Lord's Prayer: Thy kingdom come.

Word on the Cross: "Amen, I say to thee: this day thou shalt be with me in paradise."

St. Augustine: "If it is piety through which the meek are blessed, inasmuch as they shall inherit the earth; let us ask that His kingdom may come, whether it be over ourselves, that we may become meek, and not resist Him, or whether it be from heaven to earth in the splendour of the Lord's advent, in which we shall rejoice, and shall be praised, when He says, Come, you blessed of my Father, inherit the kingdom prepared for you from the foundation of the world. For in the Lord, says the prophet, shall my soul be praised; the meek shall hear thereof, and be glad." (*Sermon on the Mount*, Newman Press, pp. 125-127).

Considerations and Reflections

Holy meekness consists of gentleness and kindness, not timidity.

Courtesy.

Piety signifies reverence and godliness.

The opposing vice to meekness is anger.

The soul can not receive the Word of God except it be meek. Then it shall offer no resistance to the first inspirations of the Lord.

Meekly and docilely submit to the Will of the Lord, without resistance, without hesitation or doubt.

But the meek shall inherit the land, and shall delight in abundance of peace (Ps. 36:11).

He will guide the mild in judgment: he will teach the meek his ways (Ps. 24:9).

God hath overturned the thrones of proud princes, and hath set up the meek in their stead (Ecclus. 10:17).

For Moses was a man exceeding meek above all men that dwelt upon earth (Num. 12:3).

How to Pray the Secret Rosary

O Lord, remember David, and all his meekness (Ps. 131:1).

But the prayer of the humble and the meek hath always pleased thee (Judith 9:16).

Wherefore casting away all uncleanness, and abundance of naughtiness, with meekness receive the ingrafted word, which is able to save your souls (Ja. 1:21).

My son, do thy works in meekness, and thou shalt be beloved above the glory of men (Ecclus. 3:19).

The spirit of the Lord is upon me, because the Lord hath anointed me: he hath sent me to preach to the meek, to heal the contrite of heart, and to preach a release to the captives, and deliverance to them that are shut up (Is. 61:1).

Take up my yoke upon you, and learn of me, because I am meek, and humble of heart: and you shall find rest to your souls (Mt. 11:29).

The gentle – those who defeat Satan as the Lord teaches us to do: by forgiveness, by turning away from temptation, by loving our enemies, but truly forgiving the injuries done to us, rather than by seeking revenge.

♦♦♦

How to Pray the Secret Rosary

Personal reflections on meekness:

How to Pray the Secret Rosary

Personal reflections on meekness:

How to Pray the Secret Rosary

Chapter Three

The Third "Hail Mary"

Sorrow for Sin

Gift: Knowledge.

Beatitude: Blessed are they that mourn for they shall be comforted.

Lord's Prayer: Thy will be done on earth as it is in heaven.

Word on the Cross: "Woman, behold thy son." To the disciple, "Behold your mother."

St. Augustine: If it is knowledge through which those who mourn are blessed, inasmuch as they shall be comforted; let us pray that His will may be done as in heaven so in earth, because when the body, which is as it were the earth, shall agree in a final and complete peace with the soul, which is as it were heaven, we shall not mourn: for there is no other mourning belonging to this present time, except when these contend against each other, and compel us to say, I see another law in my members, warring against the law of my mind; and to testify our grief with tearful voice, O wretched man that I am! Who shall deliver me from the body of this death? (*Sermon on the Mount*, Newman Press, pp. 125-127).

~ ~ ~

Considerations and Reflections

Sorrow in the knowledge of our sins, as we learn God's Will.

Man has received the knowledge of good and evil. It is good to obey God, and to believe in Him, and to keep His commandment, and this is the life of man; as not to obey God is evil, and this is his death.
(St. Irenaeus, *Against Heresies*, Bk. 4, Chap. 39; www.newadvent.org/fathers).

To proclaim the acceptable year of the Lord, and the day of vengeance of our God: to comfort all that mourn (Is. 61:2).

According to Augustine (De Civ. Dei xiv, 7, 9), "all sorrow is based on love." Now the love of charity, on which the sorrow of contrition is based, is the greatest love. Therefore the sorrow of contrition is the greatest sorrow. (St. Thomas, *Summa*, Suppl. Q. 3, a.1.)

Further, it is written (Ecclus. 5:5): "Be not without fear about sin forgiven." Therefore man should always grieve, that his sins may be forgiven him (St. Thomas, *Summa, Suppl.* Q.4 a. 1).

Knowledge: Including knowledge of our sinfulness and of God's Will for us. Knowledge of God's will and how we have come short of it by sin.

Those who mourn shall be comforted. At the Cross, The Blessed Mother and St. John console each other as they mourn for the death of Jesus, a death willed by Him to redeem us from our sins.

Repentance, for not choosing the will of God.

Sins make us feel ashamed, and the memory of them serves to keep us humble (Padre Pio, *Padre Pio Teaches Us*, p. 214).

Comfort as we mourn: I know by faith that Your consolation will come, either in time or eternity, infinitely compensating for any suffering I must endure.

Compassion: A compassionate heart is one that sorrows because its brothers and sisters sorrow.

A sorrowful heart is reparation for sin (from a morning offering prayer).

And God shall wipe away all tears from their eyes: and death shall be no more, nor mourning, nor crying, nor sorrow shall be any more, for the former things are passed away (Rev. 21:4).

For the sorrow that is according to God worketh penance, steadfast unto salvation; but the sorrow of the world worketh death (2 Cor. 7:10).

Now all chastisement for the present indeed seemeth not to bring with it joy, but sorrow: but afterwards it will yield, to them that are exercised by it, the most peaceable fruit of justice (Heb. 12:11).

Not every one that saith to me, Lord, Lord, shall enter into the kingdom of heaven: but he that doth the will of my Father who is in heaven, he shall enter into the kingdom of heaven (Mt. 7:21).

Knowledge of the Will of God leads to sorrow for sin.

♦♦♦

How to Pray the Secret Rosary

Personal reflections on sorrow for sin:

How to Pray the Secret Rosary

Personal reflections on sorrow for sin:

Chapter Four

The Fourth "Hail Mary"

Faith

Gift: Fortitude.

Beatitude: Blessed are they that hunger and thirst after justice for they shall have their fill.

Lord's Prayer: Give us this day our daily bread.

Word on the Cross: "My God, my God, why hast thou forsaken me?"

St. Augustine: "If it is fortitude through which those are blessed who hunger and thirst after righteousness, inasmuch as they shall be filled; let us pray that our daily bread may be given to us today, by which, supported and sustained, we may be able to reach that most abundant fullness." (*Sermon on the Mount*, Newman Press, pp. 125-127).

~ ~ ~

Considerations and Reflections

Faith: Fortitude, justice, trust.

What then shall we say? That the Gentiles, who followed not after justice, have attained to justice, even the justice that is of faith (Rom. 9:30).

It is when it seems that we have been forsaken that we must gain the fortitude to persevere in our faith and trust in God.

But she that is a widow indeed, and desolate, let her trust in God, and continue in supplications and prayers night and day (1 Tim. 5:5).

Faith is the partaking in the creative power of God. We create the possibility for something we believe can come about. What we conceive of can come true if we have faith in God and do not waver. But the result of that faith must be hoped for. Faith is indeed "the substance of things hoped for" (Heb. 11:1).

"For, amen I say to you, if you have faith as a grain of mustard seed, you shall say to this mountain, Remove from hence hither, and it shall remove; and nothing shall be impossible to you." (Mt. 17:19.)

Let us seek the strength and fortitude of faith, so we may not stagger, waver or doubt.

Definition of Fortitude:
"Fortitude, enduring courage; strength of character in bearing pain with patience or in meeting danger undauntedly; a supernatural virtue strengthening a person's irascible appetite so that not even the greatest temporal risks can deter him from the pursuit of supernatural good." (Pallen [editor], *The New Catholic Dictionary*, 1929).

Definition of Faith:
"It is not merely a feeling or a suspicion or an opinion, but a firm, unshakeable adherence of the mind to a truth revealed by God. The motive of Divine faith, or the reason why be believe, is God's authority, His unfailing knowledge and truthfulness." (*Ibid.*).

Thus fortitude removes the inordinate fear that hinders faith (St. Thomas, *Summa*, II-II, Q. 4, a. 7).

And Jesus answering, said to them: "Amen, I say to you, if you shall have faith, and stagger not, not only this of the fig tree shall you do, but also if you shall say to this mountain, Take up and cast thyself into the sea, it shall be done." (Mt. 21:21.)

And immediately Jesus stretching forth his hand took hold of him, and said to him: "O thou of little faith, why didst thou doubt?" (Mt. 14:31.)

"For by grace you are saved through faith, and that not of yourselves, for it is the gift of God." (Eph. 2:8.)

Faith purifies the heart. St. Peter (Acts 15:9): "Purifying their hearts by faith."

St. Thomas Aquinas on the object of faith (*Summa*, II-II, Q. 1 a. 1): Dionysius says (Div. Nom. vii) that "faith is about the simple and everlasting truth." Now this is the First Truth. Therefore the object of faith is the First Truth.

And Jesus saith to him: "Go thy way, thy faith hath made thee whole." And immediately he saw, and followed him in the way (Mk. 10:52).

The ship of faith is buffeted by the winds of tribulation and the waves of temptations. The sail which is raised up is the Cross. The hull is the heart, which is strengthened by love.

Who answered and said: "It is written, Not in bread alone doth man live, but in every word that proceedeth from the mouth of God." (Mt. 4:4.)

And Jesus said to them: "I am the bread of life: he that cometh to me shall not hunger: and he that believeth in me shall never thirst." (Jn. 6:35.)

But that in the law no man is justified with God, it is manifest: because the just man liveth by faith (Gal. 3:11).

Therefore I say unto you, all things, whatsoever you ask when ye pray, believe that you shall receive; and they shall come unto you (Mk. 11:24).

Jesus answered, and said to them: "This is the work of God, that you believe in him whom he hath sent." (Jn. 6:29.)

We must have a positive certainty that the hour of our most desperate troubles is the time He has appointed to come to our assistance (Thomas de Saint-Laurent, *Confidence*, 1943, p. 27).

The Lord will take care of our interests provided that we are concerned for His. According as we are concerned for the things of God so will He look after our interests (*Ibid.*, p. 39).

Be you humbled therefore under the mighty hand of God, that he may exalt you in the time of visitation: Casting all your care upon him, for he hath care of you. Be sober and watch: because your adversary the devil, as a roaring lion, goeth about seeking whom he may devour. Whom resist ye, strong in faith: knowing that the same affliction befalls your brethren who are in the world. (1 Peter 5: 6-9).

Be in nothing solicitous; but in every thing, by prayer and supplication, with thanksgiving, let your petitions be made known to God (Phil. 4:6).

Be not solicitous therefore, saying, What shall we eat: or what shall we drink, or wherewith shall we be clothed? For after all these things do the heathens seek. For your Father knoweth that you have need of all these things. Seek ye therefore first the kingdom of God, and his justice, and all these things shall be added unto you. Be not therefore solicitous for tomorrow; for the morrow will be solicitous for itself. Sufficient for the day is the evil thereof (Mt. 6:31-34).

Wherefore having the loins of your mind girt up, being sober, trust perfectly in the grace which is offered you in the revelation of Jesus Christ (1 Peter 1:13).

O Lord my God, in thee have I put my trust: save me from all them that persecute me, and deliver me (Ps. 7:2).

Do you remember when Mary Magdalene said to Jesus: "Lord if you had been here my brother would not have died!" Almost as if He would not have been able to heal him from afar. Instead, listen to the centurion who said: "Lord I am not worthy that you should enter under my roof, only say but the word and my son shall be healed!" This indeed, is Faith! (Padre Pio, *Padre Pio Teaches Us*, p. 80.)

For the eyes of the Lord behold all the earth, and give strength to those who with a perfect heart trust in him (2 Chron. 16:9).

♦♦♦

How to Pray the Secret Rosary

Personal reflections on faith:

How to Pray the Secret Rosary

Personal reflections on faith:

Chapter Five

The Fifth "Hail Mary"

Hope

Gift: Counsel.

Beatitude: Blessed are the merciful, for they shall obtain mercy.

Lord's Prayer: And forgive us our trespasses as we forgive those who trespass against us.

Word on the Cross: "I thirst!"

St. Augustine: "If it is prudence [counsel] through which the merciful are blessed, inasmuch as they shall obtain mercy; let us forgive their debts to our debtors, and let us pray that ours may be forgiven to us." (*Sermon on the Mount*, Newman Press, pp. 125-127).

St. Thomas Aquinas on the virtue of Prudence: According to St. Thomas (*Summa*, II-II: 47:8) it is its function to do three things: to take counsel, i.e. to cast about for the means suited in the particular case under consideration to reach the end of any one moral virtue; to judge soundly of the fitness of the means suggested; and, finally, to command their employment.

Considerations and Reflections

Hope: Mercy, counsel, forgiveness.

This is the reward of the humble, who ask for counsel: that they will find it with certainty and security. (Blessed Virgin Mary in *Mystical City of God, The Incarnation*, Chapter XV.195, Ven. Mary of Agreda).

Wherefore, O king, let my counsel be acceptable to thee, and redeem thou thy sins with alms, and thy iniquities with works of mercy to the poor: perhaps he will forgive thy offences (Dan. 4:24).

After walking in the darkness of abandonment, doing the will of God by faith, the soul begins to thirst for comfort – for the brighter light of hope and for the ultimate goal.

You receive as much as you hope for. Hope a lot and you will receive a lot (Padre Pio, *Padre Pio Teaches Us*, p. 103).

Behold the eyes of the Lord are on them that fear him: and on them that hope in his mercy (Ps. 32:18).

Ye that fear the Lord, hope in him: and mercy shall come to you for your delight (Ecclus. 2:9).

Go then and learn what this meaneth, I will have mercy and not sacrifice. For I am not come to call the just, but sinners (Mt. 9:13).

Blessed be the God and Father of our Lord Jesus Christ, who according to his great mercy hath regenerated us unto a lively hope, by the resurrection of Jesus Christ from the dead (1 Peter 1:3).

Jesus thirsts: for the glory of God and the salvation of souls.

Mercy triumphs over judgment.

For judgment without mercy to him that hath not done mercy. And mercy exalteth itself above judgment (Ja. 2:13).

We enter into a compact with God:
"Nor are we indeed carelessly to pass by the circumstance, that of all those sentences in which the Lord has taught us to pray, He has judged that the one chiefly to be commended has reference to the forgiveness of sins: in which He would have us to be merciful, because it is the only wisdom for escaping misery. For in no other sentence do we pray in such a way that we, as it were, enter into a compact with God: for we say, Forgive us, as we also forgive. And if we lie in that compact, the whole prayer is fruitless. For He speaks thus: For if you forgive men their trespasses, your heavenly Father will also forgive you: But if you forgive not men their trespasses, neither will your

Father forgive your trespasses." (St. Aug., *Sermon on the Mount*, bk. 2, ch. 11.)

How great is the mercy of the Lord, and his forgiveness to them that turn to him! (Ecclus. 17:28.)

Forgive, I beseech thee, the sins of this people, according to the greatness of thy mercy, as thou hast been merciful to them from their going out of Egypt unto this place (Num. 14:19).

For if you will forgive men their offences, your heavenly Father will forgive you also your offences (Mt. 6:14).

Do ye manfully, and let your heart be strengthened, all ye that hope in the Lord (Ps. 30:25).

But Christ as the Son in his own house: which house are we, if we hold fast the confidence and glory of hope unto the end (Heb. 3:6).

Confidence by itself can easily obtain all things (St. Gertrude, *Love, Peace and Joy*, TAN Books, p. 70).

♦♦♦

How to Pray the Secret Rosary

Personal reflections on hope:

How to Pray the Secret Rosary

Personal reflections on hope:

Chapter Six

The Sixth "Hail Mary"

Love

Gift: Understanding.

Beatitude: Blessed are the clean of heart for they shall see God.

Lord's Prayer: And lead us not into temptation.

Word on the Cross: "It is consummated."

St. Augustine: "If it is understanding through which the pure in heart are blessed, inasmuch as they shall see God; let us pray not to be led into temptation, lest we should have a double heart, in not seeking after a single good, to which we may refer all our actings, but at the same time pursuing things temporal and earthly. For temptations arising from those things which seem to men burdensome and calamitous, will be powerless to us, if those other temptations, which befall us through the enticements of such things as men count good and cause for rejoicing, have no power of us." (*Sermon on the Mount*, Newman Press, pp. 125-127).

Considerations and Reflections

Love: understanding, purity, resisting temptation

Consummated in love.

And being consummated, he became, to all that obey him, the cause of eternal salvation (Heb. 5:9).

And I have filled him with the spirit of God, with wisdom and understanding, and knowledge in all manner of work (Ex. 31:3).

For wisdom is more active than all active things: and reacheth everywhere by reason of her purity (Wis. 7:24).

Purity of heart – loving only God and for God, not admixing this pure love with love of creatures for their own sake.

Put an end to our love for the world, lead us to love You. True good is the source of our happiness; the good that must be loved is You Lord, not the things of this world.

The pure are able to see God, who is love – so they see what love is and are filled with it.

He that loveth not, knoweth not God: for God is charity (1 Jn. 4:8).

The pivot of perfection is charity; he who lives in charity lives in God, because God is charity, as the apostle says (Padre Pio, *Counsels*, p. 12).

Try always to advance more in charity; enlarge your heart with confidence for the divine gifts which the Holy Spirit is anxious to pour into it (*Ibid.*, p. 14).

Dearly beloved, let us love one another, for charity is of God. And every one that loveth, is born of God, and knoweth God (1 Jn. 4:7).

He who shows himself amiable in everything must necessarily make himself loved (St. Aphonsus, *Eucharist*, p. 235).

Plato said that love is the lodestone of love. Hence comes the common proverb, as St. John Chrysostom remarks: "If you wish to be loved, love," for certainly there is no more effectual means to secure for one's self the affections of another than to love him, and to make him aware that he is loved (St. Alphonsus, *Incarnation*, p. 32).

Men allow themselves to be drawn by love. The tokens of affection shown to them are a sort of chain which binds them, and in a manner forces them to love those who love them (*Ibid.*, p. 19).

For a true lover not only cherishes his beloved more than himself but in a certain sense he becomes oblivious of himself on account of the one he loves (Anonymous, *Cloud of Unknowing*, p. 87).

And that he should be loved with the whole heart, and with the whole understanding, and with the whole soul, and with the whole strength; and to love one's neighbour as one's self, is a greater thing than all holocausts and sacrifices (Mark 12:33).

Son, when thou comest to the service of God, stand in justice and in fear, and prepare thy soul for temptation (Ecclus. 2:1).

And because thou wast acceptable to God, it was necessary that temptation should prove thee (Tob. 12:13).

Let no temptation take hold on you, but such as is human. And God is faithful, who will not suffer you to be tempted above that which you are able: but will make also with temptation issue, that you may be able to bear it (1 Cor. 10:13).

A pure soul is synonymous with a heart full of love of God (Padre Pio, *Counsels*, p. 8).

It is not a sin merely to have impure thoughts; dispelling them is an act of virtue (Padre Pio, *Ibid.*, p. 28).

Charity is the queen of virtues. As the pearls are held together by the thread, thus the virtues by charity; and as the pearls fall when the thread breaks, thus the virtues are lost if charity diminishes (Padre Pio, *Ibid.*, p. 14).

He who offends God in charity, offends the pupil of His eye. Charity, my son, is the pupil of God's eye.
Without charity you can't please God (Padre Pio, *Padre Pio Teaches Us*, p. 38).

◆◆◆

How to Pray the Secret Rosary

Personal reflections on love:

How to Pray the Secret Rosary

Personal reflections on love:

How to Pray the Secret Rosary

Chapter Seven

The Seventh "Hail Mary"

Abandonment

Gift: Wisdom.

Beatitude: Blessed are the peacemakers for they shall be called children of God.

Lord's Prayer: But deliver us from evil.

Word on the Cross: "Father, into thy hands I commend my spirit."

St. Augustine: "If it is wisdom through which the peacemakers are blessed, inasmuch as they shall be called the children of God; let us pray that we may be freed from evil, for that very freedom will make us free, *i.e.* sons of God, so that we may cry in the spirit of adoption, 'Abba, Father.'" (*Sermon on the Mount*, Newman Press, pp. 125-127).

Considerations and Reflections

Abandonment: perseverance, wisdom, peace.

What God arranges for us to experience at each moment is the best and holiest thing that could happen to us (Caussade, *Abandonment to Divine Providence*, p. 27.)

As God wants to look after all our affairs, let us leave them all to him so that we can concentrate our whole attention on him (Caussade, *Abandonment to Divine Providence*, p. 52).

Behold, O my God and Creator, the offering I make of my entire being – I submit my will entirely to Thine, dispose of me as Thou wouldst in life and in death, in time or eternity. (Dom Lorenzo Scupoli, *The Spiritual Combat*, TAN Books, p. 174.)

When we completely abandon and surrender ourselves to God we will experience the peace of Christ.

Let us abandon ourselves into God's hands ever more because there is precious little to hope for from man (Padre Pio, *Padre Pio Teaches Us*, p. 104).

Final Perseverance:

Wherefore, brethren, labour the more, that by good works you may make sure your calling and election (2 Peter 1:10).

Of all the virtues, perseverance alone is crowned (St. Bernard, cited in Cardinal Cushing, *Eternal Thoughts*, vol. 2 p. 234).

Persevere under discipline. God dealeth with you as with his sons; for what son is there, whom the father doth not correct? (Heb. 12:7.)

And you shall be hated by all men for my name's sake: but he that shall persevere unto the end, he shall be saved (Mt. 10:22).

Know ye that the Lord will hear your prayers, if you continue with perseverance in fastings and prayers in the sight of the Lord (Judith 4:11).

The soul's final peace comes from total surrender to the Will of God.

For this is the will of God, your sanctification (1 Thes. 4:3).

When there is an end to our own will there is no such thing as hell (St. Bernard, cited in *The Heliotropium,* p. 215).

This have I determined in My Heart, Child, that the greatest Sacrament, the Holy Eucharist, should impart the greatest grace – perseverance (Arnoudt p. 677).

~ ~ ~

"Daughter, the most beautiful act, and most pleasing to Me, is the abandonment in My Will – but so great, that the soul would remember no more that her being exists; rather, everything for her is Divine Will. Even though sorrow for one's own sins is good and praiseworthy, yet, it does not destroy one's own being; while abandoning oneself completely in My Will destroys one's own being, and makes one reacquire the Divine Being." (Luisa Piccarreta, *Book of Heaven*, Vol. 8, 06/23/1917.)

"See, then, how complete abandonment in Me is necessary in order to live in My Will." (*Ibid.*, Vol. 16, 02/10/1924).

"And then, the soul places herself in her true nothingness - not in humility, in which she always feels something of herself. And, as a nothing, she enters into the All, and she operates with Me, in Me and like Me - completely stripped of herself, not caring about merit or self-interest, but all intent only on making Me content, giving Me absolute lordship over her acts, without even wanting to know what I do with them." (*Ibid.*, Vol. 12, 12/06/1917).

♦♦♦

How to Pray the Secret Rosary

Personal reflections on abandonment:

Personal reflections on abandonment:

Chapter Eight

The Father

The Father is the Creator. "I believe in one God, the Father almighty, maker of heaven and earth, and of all things visible and invisible." (Creed of the Mass).

Behold the birds of the air, for they neither sow, nor do they reap, nor gather into barns: and your heavenly Father feedeth them. Are not you of much more value than they? (Mt. 6:26.)

We are also correct in giving the name Father to this one Lord our God, since He has regenerated us through His grace (St. Augustine, *The Trinity*, Cath. U. Press, p. 189).

Jesus is "of one being with the Father: by whom all things were made." (Creed of the Mass).

The Father is the Principle of the whole Deity (St. Augustine, *ibid.*, p. 168).

Wisdom refers to the intellect:

God endowed man with the faculties and powers of memory, intellect, and will. The intellect can be said by accommodation to pertain to the Father, because by our intellect we can know something of Him by our knowledge of the Creation. God makes himself known by what He has created, since He created all things for man, and to show His love for man.

The Father Himself is Wisdom (St. Augustine, *ibid.*, p. 228).

Truth sees God, and wisdom contemplates God, and from these two comes a third, a holy and wonderful delight in God, who is love (Julian of Norwich, *Revelations*, p. 102).

But the hour cometh, and now is, when the true adorers shall adore the Father in spirit and in truth. For the Father also seeketh such to adore him (Jn. 4:23).

Be you therefore perfect, as also your heavenly Father is perfect (Mt. 5:48).

Blessed be the God and Father of our Lord Jesus Christ, who hath blessed us with spiritual blessings in heavenly places, in Christ (Eph. 1:3).

Giving thanks to God the Father, who hath made us worthy to be partakers of the lot of the saints in light (Col. 1:12).

Religion clean and undefiled before God and the Father, is this: to visit the fatherless and widows in their tribulation: and to keep one' s self unspotted from this world (Ja. 1:27).

He shall cry out to me: Thou art my Father: my God, and the support of my salvation (Ps. 88:27).

But God is the Father of the Son from eternity; while He is the Father of the creature in time. Therefore paternity in God is taken in a personal sense as regards the Son, before it is so taken as regards the creature (St. Thomas, *Summa*, I: Q. 33, a. 3).

The Father is unbegotten:
In every genus there must be something first; so in the divine nature there must be some one principle which is not from another, and which we call "unbegotten." (St. Thomas, *Summa*, I: Q. 33, a. 4).

But of that day and hour no one knoweth, not the angels of heaven, but the Father alone (Mt. 24:36).

~ ~ ~

"The eternal Father, as faith teaches us, is the fount and origin of the other persons of the Trinity. Thus the Father communicates to the Son and Holy Ghost His entire nature without division, retaining His own proper personality uncommunicated. Admire and adore this most profound mystery, exercise your faith in acts upon it, and acknowledge the weakness of the human intellect in attempting to comprehend the immensity of the Divinity. Say with St. Paul, 'Oh, the depth of the riches of the wisdom and of the knowledge of God!' (Rom. 11:33.)

"Although all the external works of God are common to the three persons of the Trinity, the works of omnipotence, nevertheless, are said to belong to the Father; such are creation, preservation, and providence. Hence, you should learn how much you ought to love that Being, who has created you, who preserves you, and who for your sake has formed this admirable world. Learn too, how much reason you have to fear that Being, who is able to destroy both soul and body in hell.

"This eternal Father, so great and incomprehensible, has stooped so low beneath Himself for love of His poor insignificant vassals, as to condescend to make us His adopted children and heirs of heaven. The 'Father Himself loves you', says Christ (Jn. 16:27), nay more, 'God so loved the world that He gave His only begotten Son.' (Jn. 3:16.) Remember, then, what great reason you have to love and honor with your whole heart, so loving a Father. You cannot love and honor Him unless you avoid whatever is displeasing to Him, and do that which is pleasing to Him; that is, unless you avoid evil and do good."

(Cardinal Cushing, *Eternal Thoughts*, Vol. 1, p. 231-2).

~ ~ ~

How to Pray the Secret Rosary

Excerpts from the Catechism of the Council of Trent

Why God is called "Father" (TAN Books, pp. 20-21):

God Is Called Father Because He Is Creator And Ruler

Even some on whose darkness the light of faith never shone conceived God to be an eternal substance from whom all things have their beginning, and by whose Providence they are governed and preserved in their order and state of existence. Since, therefore, he to whom a family owes its origin and by whose wisdom and authority it is governed is called *father*, so by analogy derived from human things these persons gave the name *Father* to God, whom they acknowledge to be the Creator and Governor of the universe. The Sacred Scriptures also, when they wish to show that to God must be ascribed the creation of all things, supreme power and admirable Providence, make use of the same name. Thus we read: *Is not he thy Father, that hath possessed thee, and made thee and created thee?* And: *Have we not all one Father? hath not one God created us?*

God Is Called Father Because He Adopts Christians Through Grace

But God, particularly in the New Testament, is much more frequently, and in some sense peculiarly, called the Father of Christians, *who have not received* *the spirit of bondage again in fear; but have received the spirit of adoption of sons (*of God*), whereby they cry: Abba (Father). For the Father hath bestowed upon us that manner of charity that we should be called, and be the sons of God, and if sons, heirs also; heirs indeed of God, and joint heirs with Christ, who is the firstborn amongst many brethren, and is not ashamed to call us brethren.* Whether, therefore, we look to the common title of creation and Providence, or to the special one of spiritual adoption, rightly do the faithful profess their belief that God is their Father.

The Name Father Also Discloses The Plurality Of Persons In God

But the pastor should teach that on hearing the word *Father*, besides the ideas already unfolded, the mind should rise to more exalted mysteries. Under the name *Father*, the divine oracles begin to unveil to us a mysterious truth which is more abstruse and more deeply hidden in that inaccessible light in which God dwells, and which human reason and understanding could not attain to, nor even conjecture to exist.

This name implies that in the one Essence of the Godhead is proposed to our belief, not only one Person, but a distinction of persons; for in one Divine Nature there are Three Persons the Father, begotten of none; the Son, begotten of the Father before all ages; the Holy Ghost, proceeding from the Father and the likewise, from all eternity.

♦♦♦

How to Pray the Secret Rosary

Personal reflections on God the Father

How to Pray the Secret Rosary

Personal reflections on God the Father

Chapter Nine

The Son

It is written (1 Peter 1:18): "You were not redeemed with corruptible things as gold or silver from your vain conversation of the tradition of your fathers: but with the precious blood of Christ, as of a lamb unspotted and undefiled." And (Gal. 3:13): "Christ hath redeemed us from the curse of the law, being made a curse for us." Now He is said to be a curse for us inasmuch as He suffered upon the tree, as stated above (Question 46, Article 4). Therefore He did redeem us by His Passion. (St. Thomas, *Summa*, III, Q. 48, a. 4.)

And she shall bring forth a son: and thou shalt call his name Jesus, for he shall save his people from their sins (Mt. 1:21).

Wherefore with regard to Our Lord Jesus Christ we hold . . . that the Son of God is understood to be equal to the Father according to the form of God in which He is, and less than the Father according to the form of a slave the He has received (St. Augustine, *The Trinity*, p. 52).

Some things in the Scriptures concerning the Father and the Son are, therefore, put in such a way as to indicate the unity and equality of the substance of the Father and the Son, as, for example: "I and the Father are One," and "When he was in the form of God He thought it not robbery to be equal to God," and whatever other texts there are of a similar nature; but some are so put as to show that the Son is less on account of the form of a slave, that is, on account of the creature with a changeable and human substance that He assumed, such as "For the Father is greater than I." (St. Augustine, *ibid.,* p. 53).

For neither doth the Father judge any man, but hath given all judgment to the Son (Jn. 5:22).

The Lord hath said to me: Thou art my son, this day have I begotten thee. Ask of me, and I will give thee the Gentiles for thy inheritance, and the utmost parts of the earth for thy possession (Psalm 2:7-8).

And behold a voice from heaven, saying: This is my beloved Son, in whom I am well pleased (Mt. 3:17).

But he held his peace, and answered nothing. Again the high priest asked him, and said to him: Art thou the Christ the Son of the blessed God? And Jesus said to him: I am. And you shall see the Son of man sitting on the right hand of the power of God, and coming with the clouds of heaven (Mk. 14: 61-62).

In this is charity: not as though we had loved God, but because he hath first loved us, and sent his Son to be a propitiation for our sins (1 Jn. 4:10).

Whosoever shall confess that Jesus is the Son of God, God abideth in him, and he in God (1 John 4:15).

From the morning watch even until night, let Israel hope in the Lord. Because with the Lord there is mercy: and with him plentiful redemption. And he shall redeem Israel from all his iniquities. (Psalm 129; 6-8).

~ ~ ~

"He is properly the Word (or idea) of the divine intellect expressing in Himself the substance of the divine nature. The Word became vocal by the mystery of the Incarnation, and declared to mankind the secrets of His Father. Who shall declare his generation, exclaims the prophet (Is. 53:8). Neither the angels themselves, nor all the eloquence of men can explain His mysterious birth. If they could, this divine Word would present no object for our faith, because our understanding, which would then be capable of comprehending His divine nature, must either be infinite, or this divine Word must be a limited and imperfect Being. Our understanding is not infinite, and He is not an imperfect Being; therefore, we cannot comprehend this mysterious generation by any faculty we possess. It suffices that we adore Him with an unshaken faith, and rejoice in His glory, which is substantially equal to the glory of His Father.

"This only-begotten Son of God loved the world to such a degree, that He gave His life to redeem it. God became man, writes St. Augustine, that we might become God, and the eloquent St. Leo remarks, 'Christ was made the son of man, that we might be made the sons of God.' O ineffable and incomprehensible mystery!

"Love that sacred humanity which the Son of God assumed, and which was nailed to the cross for your sake. Say with the devout St. Bernard, 'The more vile this Son of God has become for my sake, by so much the more is He dear to me.' Do not alienate His affections by sinning against Him."

(Cardinal Cushing, *Eternal Thoughts*, Vol. 1, p. 233-4).

~ ~ ~

Excerpts from the Catechism of the Council of Trent

"Jesus Christ, His Only Son, Our Lord, Who was Conceived by the Holy Ghost, Born of the Virgin Mary" (TAN Books, pp. 33-45):

Jesus

Jesus is the proper name of the Godman and signifies Saviour: a name given Him not accidentally, or by the judgment or will of man, but by the counsel and command of God. For the Angel announced to Mary His mother: *Behold thou shalt conceive in thy womb, and shalt bring forth a son; and thou shalt call his name Jesus.* He afterwards not only commanded Joseph, who was espoused to the Virgin, to call the child by that name, but also declared the reason why He should be so called. *Joseph, son of David,* said the Angel, *fear not to take unto thee Mary thy wife, for that which is conceived in her is of the Holy Ghost. And she shall bring forth a son and thou shalt call his name Jesus. For he shall save his people from their sins.*

Christ

To the name *Jesus* is added that of *Christ*, which signifies *the anointed*. This name is expressive of honour and office, and is not peculiar to one thing only, but common to many; for in the Old Law priests and kings, whom God, on account of the dignity of their office, commanded to he anointed, were called christs.

When Jesus Christ our Saviour came into the world, He assumed these three characters of Prophet, Priest and King, and was therefore called *Christ*, having been anointed for the discharge of these functions, not by mortal hand or with earthly ointment, but by the power of His heavenly Father and with a spiritual oil; for the plenitude of the Holy Spirit and a more copious effusion of all gifts than any other created being is capable of receiving were poured into His soul.

His Only Son

In these words, mysteries more exalted with regard to Jesus are proposed to the faithful as objects of their belief and contemplation; namely, that He is the Son of God, and true God, like the Father who begot Him from eternity. We also confess that He is the

Second Person of the Blessed Trinity, equal in all things to the Father and the Holy Ghost; for in the Divine Persons nothing unequal or unlike should exist, or even be imagined to exist, since we acknowledge the essence, will and power of all to be one. This truth is both clearly revealed in many passages of Holy Scripture and sublimely announced in the testimony of St. John: *In the beginning was the Word, and the Word was with God, and the Word was God.*

It is better, however, to contemplate what faith proposes, and in the sincerity of our souls to believe and confess that Jesus Christ is true God and true Man, as God, begotten of the Father before all ages, as Man, born in time of Mary, His Virgin Mother.

While we thus acknowledge His twofold Nativity; we believe Him to be one Son, because His divine and human natures meet in one Person.

Our Lord

He humbled himself, becoming obedient unto death, even to the death of the cross. For which cause God also hath exalted him, and hath given him a name which is above all names: that at the name of Jesus every knee should bend, of those that are in heaven, on earth, and under the earth: and that every tongue should confess that the Lord Jesus Christ is in the glory of God the Father. And of Himself He said, after His Resurrection: *All power is given to me in heaven and in earth.*

He is also called *Lord* because in one Person both natures, the human and the divine, are united; and even though He had not died for us, He would have yet deserved, by this admirable union, to be constituted common Lord of all created things, particularly of the faithful who obey and serve Him with all the fervour of their souls.

Who was Conceived

And the Word was made flesh and dwelt among us. The Word, which is a Person of the Divine Nature, assumed human nature in such a manner that there should be one and the same Person in both the divine and human natures. Hence this admirable union preserved the actions and properties of both natures; and as Pope St. Leo the Great said: *The lowliness of the inferior nature was not consumed in the glory of the superior, nor did the assumption of the inferior lessen the glory of the superior.*

By the Holy Ghost

Although the Son only assumed human nature, yet all the Persons of the Trinity, the Father, the Son, and the Holy Ghost, were authors of this mystery. It is a principle of Christian faith that whatever God does outside Himself in creation is common to the Three Persons, and that one neither does more than, nor acts without another.

Again – and this should overwhelm us with astonishment – as soon as the soul of Christ was united to His body, the Divinity became united to both; and thus at the same time His body was formed and animated, and the Divinity united to body and soul.

Hence, at the same instant He was perfect God and perfect man, and the most Holy Virgin, having at the same moment conceived God and man, is truly and properly called Mother of God and man.

Born of the Virgin Mary

The words of the Angel who first announced the happy tidings to the world declare with what joy and delight of soul this mystery of our faith should be meditated upon. *Behold*, said the Angel, *I bring you good tidings of great joy that shall be to all the people.* The same sentiments are clearly conveyed in the song chanted by the heavenly host: *Glory to God in the highest; and on earth peace to men of good will.* Then began the fulfilment of the splendid promise made by God to Abraham, that in his seed *all the nations of the earth should one day be blessed*; for Mary, whom we truly proclaim and venerate as Mother of God, because she brought forth Him who is at once God and man, was descended from King David.

◆◆◆

How to Pray the Secret Rosary

Personal reflections on God the Son

How to Pray the Secret Rosary

Personal reflections on God the Son

Chapter Ten

The Holy Spirit

The Holy Spirit is the Sanctifier.

That I [St. Paul] should be the minister of Christ Jesus among the Gentiles; sanctifying the gospel of God, that the oblation of the Gentiles may be made acceptable and sanctified in the Holy Ghost (Rom. 15:16).

According to the foreknowledge of God the Father, unto the sanctification of the Spirit, unto obedience and sprinkling of the blood of Jesus Christ: Grace unto you and peace be multiplied (1 Peter 1:2).

And such some of you were; but you are washed, but you are sanctified, but you are justified in the name of our Lord Jesus Christ, and the Spirit of our God (1 Cor. 6:11).

Sanctify them in truth; Thy word is truth (John 17:17).

For this is the will of God, your sanctification (1 Thes. 4:3).

And grieve not the holy Spirit of God: whereby you are sealed unto the day of redemption (Eph. 4:30).

Ask God for his seven gifts. May the virtue of perseverance and the holy fear of God make us turn away from sin and practice virtue (Padre Pio, *Padre Pio Teaches Us*, p. 101).

Being exalted therefore by the right hand of God, and having received of the Father the promise of the Holy Ghost, he hath poured forth this which you see and hear (Acts 2:33).

Wherefore I give you to understand, that no man, speaking by the Spirit of God, saith Anathema to Jesus. And no man can say the Lord Jesus, but by the Holy Ghost (1 Cor. 12:3).

And Jesus being baptized, forthwith came out of the water: and lo, the heavens were opened to him: and he saw the Spirit of God descending as a dove, and coming upon him (Mt. 3:16).

I say then, walk in the spirit, and you shall not fulfill the lusts of the flesh. For the flesh lusteth against the spirit: and the spirit against the flesh; for these are contrary one to another: so that you do not the things that you would. But if you are led by the spirit, you are not under the law. (Gal. 5: 16-18.)

But when he, the Spirit of truth, is come, he will teach you all truth. For he shall not speak of himself; but what things soever he shall hear, he shall speak; and the things that are to come, he shall shew you (John 16:13).

Which in other generations was not known to the sons of men, as it is now revealed to his holy apostles and prophets in the Spirit (Eph. 3:5).

Indwelling of the Spirit:

And I will give you a new heart, and put a new spirit within you: and I will take away the stony heart out of your flesh, and will give you a heart of flesh. And I will put my spirit in the midst of you: and I will cause you to walk in my commandments, and to keep my judgments, and do them (Ezk. 36:26-27).

Know you not, that you are the temple of God, and that the Spirit of God dwelleth in you? (1 Cor. 3:16.)

For whosoever are led by the Spirit of God, they are the sons of God (Rom. 8:14).

But you are not in the flesh, but in the spirit, if so be that the Spirit of God dwell in you. Now if any man have not the Spirit of Christ, he is none of his (Rom. 8:9).

The spirit of the Lord is upon me, because the Lord hath anointed me: he hath sent me to preach to the meek, to heal the contrite of heart, and to preach a release to the captives, and deliverance to them that are shut up (Is. 61:1; Lk. 4:18).

"The Holy Ghost appeared over Christ in the form of a dove, both to teach us His love, in regard to those whom Christ came to redeem, for the dove is an emblem of social love, and to inspire us with mildness and simplicity of life and action. To him are attributed the works of justification, the distribution of graces, and the benefits of inspiration. The wind blows where it will, and thou hearest its sound but dost not know where it comes from of where it goes (Jn. 3:8). Pray with earnestness and fervor for this divine grace, for without it, it is impossible to perform a supernatural meritorious act.

"Honor and reverence this divine Person, and join your voice with that of the angels and saints, crying out "Holy, Holy, Holy Lord God of Hosts.

"Hence, St. Paul writes to his Corinthian converts, 'Do you not know that your members are the temple of the Holy Spirit, who is in you, whom you have from God, and that you are not your own?' (1 Cor. 6:19). Take care, then, that you never profane His temple. Beg of Him, by continued prayer, that He wash away what is unclean in you, water what is dry, heal what is wounded, bend what is stubborn, warm what is cold, and correct all your deviations."

(Cardinal Cushing, *Eternal Thoughts*, Vol. 1, p. 235-6).

~ ~ ~

How to Pray the Secret Rosary

Excerpts from the Catechism of the Council of Trent

I believe in the Holy Ghost (TAN Books, pp: 89-95):

Holy Ghost

No one should be surprised that a proper name is not given to the Third, as to the First and Second Persons... Hence we cannot discover a proper name to express the manner in which God communicates Himself entire, by the force of His love. Wherefore we call the Third Person *Holy Ghost*, a name, however, peculiarly appropriate to Him who infuses into us spiritual life, and without whose holy inspiration we can do nothing meritorious of eternal life.

The Holy Ghost Is Equal To The Father And The Son

Finally, what most strongly confirms this truth is the fact that Holy Scripture assigns to the Holy Ghost whatever attributes we believe proper to God. Wherefore to Him is ascribed the honour of temples, as when the Apostle says: *Know you not that your members are the temple of the Holy Ghost?* Scripture also attributes to Him the power to sanctify, to vivify, to search the depths of God, to speak by the Prophets, and to be present in all places, all of which can be attributed to God alone.

The Holy Ghost Is Distinct From The Father And Son

To say nothing of other testimonies of Scripture, the form of Baptism, taught by our Redeemer, shows most clearly that the Holy Ghost is the Third Person, self existent in the Divine Nature and distinct from the other Persons. It is a doctrine taught also by the Apostle when he says: *The grace of our Lord Jesus Christ, and the charity of God, and the communication of the Holy Ghost, be with you all. Amen.*

Certain Divine Works are Appropriated to the Holy Ghost

Although the intrinsic works of the most Holy Trinity are common to the Three Persons, yet many of them are attributed specially to the Holy Ghost, to signify that they arise from the boundless charity of God towards us. For as the Holy Ghost proceeds from the divine will, inflamed, as it were, with love, we can perceive that these effects which are referred particularly to the Holy Ghost, are the result of God's supreme love for us.

Hence it is that the Holy Ghost is called a *gift*; for by the word *gift* we understand that which is kindly and gratuitously bestowed, without expectation of any return. Whatever gifts and graces, therefore, have been conferred on us by God – *and what have we,* says the Apostle, *that we have not received from God?* – we should piously and gratefully acknowledge as bestowed by the grace and gift of the Holy Ghost.

The Seven Gifts

The Prophet (Isaias), however, enumerates the chief effects which are most properly ascribed to the Holy Ghost: *The spirit of wisdom and understanding, the spirit of counsel and fortitude, the spirit of knowledge and piety, and the spirit of the fear of the Lord.* These effects are called the gifts of the Holy Ghost, and sometimes they are even called the Holy Ghost. Wisely, therefore, does St. Augustine admonish us, whenever we meet the word Holy Ghost in Scripture, to distinguish whether it means the Third Person of the Trinity or His gifts and operations.' The two are as far apart as the Creator is from the creature.

♦♦♦

How to Pray the Secret Rosary

Personal reflections on God the Holy Spirit

How to Pray the Secret Rosary

Personal reflections on God the Holy Spirit

How to Pray the Secret Rosary

Chapter 11

Praying the traditional Rosary

The traditional fifteen decade Marian Rosary is a complete Rosary, comprising the five Joyful, five Sorrowful, five and Glorious mysteries as bequeathed to the Church by the Blessed Virgin herself.

There is an enduring Catholic tradition that the original fifteen mysteries of the Rosary were revealed by our Holy Mother to St. Dominic, and later Blessed Alan de la Roche re-established this devotion.

Each of the three categories – joyful, sorrowful, and glorious – is composed of five mysteries, thus totaling fifteen mysteries in all.

[This book is concerned with the mysteries of the Rosary traditionally bequeathed to us by the Blessed Virgin herself. In 2002 Pope John Paul II wrote that one may add five *optional* luminous mysteries, the praying of which is "left to the freedom of individuals and communities." (*Rosarium Virginis Marae*, no. 19, www.vatican.va)].

~~~

The five joyful mysteries:

1. **The Annunciation**
   Mary consents to be the Mother of God.

How to Pray the Secret Rosary

2. **The Visitation**
   Mary visits her cousin Elizabeth.
3. **The Nativity**
   Jesus is born in a stable in Bethlehem.
4. **The Presentation**
   Mary and Joseph present Jesus to God in the Temple.
5. **The Finding of Jesus in the Temple**
   Mary and Joseph find Jesus in the Temple.

The five sorrowful mysteries:

1. **The Agony in the Garden**
   Jesus in the Garden of Gethsemane.
2. **The Scourging at the Pillar**
   Jesus is cruelly whipped.
3. **The Crowning With Thorns**
   Jesus is mocked and crowned with thorns.
4. **The Carrying of the Cross**
   Jesus carries His cross.
5. **The Crucifixion**
   Jesus, nailed to the cross, dies.

The five glorious mysteries

- **The Resurrection**
  Jesus is raised from the dead.
- **The Ascension**
  Jesus returns to heaven.

How to Pray the Secret Rosary

- **The Coming of the Holy Spirit**
  The Holy Spirit descends upon the disciples and Mary.
- **The Assumption of Mary**
  Mary is taken body and soul into heaven.
- **The Coronation of Mary**
  Mary is crowned Queen of Heaven and Earth.

When praying the Rosary, one prays ten Hail Mary prayers for each mystery, while meditating on it. A complete Rosary consists of all fifteen mysteries, but often only one category of five mysteries is prayed in a day. The typical way a Rosary is prayed is as follows:

- Make the Sign of the Cross and pray the Apostles Creed [the words for the Apostles Creed and the other prayers follow this section].

- Pray one Our Father, three Hail Marys, and one Glory Be.

- Call to mind the first mystery you are praying, and pray one Our Father, ten Hail Marys, and one Glory Be, followed by the Fatima prayer.

- Repeat the prior step for each mystery until you pray all of the mysteries that you intend to pray. Usually this would be five, ten or fifteen mysteries.

- Conclude with the Hail Holy Queen.

How to Pray the Secret Rosary

The Prayers which comprise the Rosary

The Sign of the Cross
In the name of the Father of the Son and of the Holy Spirit. Amen

The Apostle's Creed

I believe in God, the Father Almighty, Creator of Heaven and earth; and in Jesus Christ, His only Son, Our Lord, Who was conceived by the Holy Ghost, born of the Virgin Mary, suffered under Pontius Pilate, was crucified; died, and was buried. He descended into Hell; the third day He arose again from the dead; He ascended into Heaven, sitteth at the right hand of God, the Father Almighty; from thence He shall come to judge the living and the dead. I believe in the Holy Spirit, the holy Catholic Church, the communion of saints, the forgiveness of sins, the resurrection of the body, and the life everlasting. Amen.

The Our Father

Our Father, Who art in heaven, hallowed be Thy name; Thy kingdom come; Thy will be done on earth as it is in heaven. Give us this day our daily bread; and forgive us our trespasses as we forgive those who trespass against us; and lead us not into temptation, but deliver us from evil. Amen.

How to Pray the Secret Rosary

Hail Mary

Hail Mary, full of grace. The Lord is with thee. Blessed art thou amongst women, and blessed is the fruit of thy womb, Jesus. Holy Mary, Mother of God, pray for us sinners, now and at the hour of our death, Amen.

Glory Be

Glory be to the Father, and to the Son, and to the Holy Spirit, as it was in the beginning, is now, and ever shall be, world without end. Amen.

Fatima Prayer

O my Jesus, forgive us our sins. Save us from the fires of hell. Lead all souls into heaven, especially those in most need of thy mercy.

Hail Holy Queen

Hail, holy Queen, Mother of mercy, our life, our sweetness and our hope. To thee do we cry, poor banished children of Eve: to thee do we send up our sighs, mourning and weeping in this valley of tears. Turn then, most gracious Advocate, thine eyes of mercy toward us, and after this our exile, show unto us the blessed fruit of thy womb, Jesus. O clement, O loving, O sweet Virgin Mary! Pray for us O Holy Mother of God, That we may be worthy of the promises of Christ. (Optional:)

How to Pray the Secret Rosary

O God whose only begotten Son by his life, death, and Resurrection has purchased for us the rewards of eternal life; grant we beseech thee, that meditating on these mysteries of the Most Holy Rosary of the Blessed Virgin Mary, we may imitate what they contain and obtain what they promise through the same Christ our Lord. Amen.

The Fifteen Promises of Mary Granted to those who Recite the Rosary

I. Whoever shall faithfully serve me by the recitation of the Rosary, shall receive signal graces.

II. I promise my special protection and the greatest graces to all those who shall recite the Rosary.

III. The Rosary shall be a powerful armor against hell, it will destroy vice, decrease sin, and defeat heresies.

IV. It will cause virtue and good works to flourish; it will obtain for souls the abundant mercy of God; it will withdraw the heart of men from the love of the world and its vanities, and will lift them to the desire of eternal things. Oh, that souls would sanctify themselves by this means.

V. The soul which recommend itself to me by the recitation of the Rosary, shall not perish.

VI. Whoever shall recite the Rosary devoutly, applying himself to the consideration of its sacred mysteries shall never be conquered by misfortune. God will not chastise him in His justice, he shall die an unprovided death; if he be just he shall remain in the grace of God, and become worthy of eternal life.

VII. Whoever shall have a true devotion for the Rosary shall not die without the sacraments of the Church.

VIII. Those who are faithful to recite the Rosary shall have during their life and at their death the light of God and the plenitude of His graces; at the moment of death they shall participate in the merits of the saints in paradise.

IX. I shall deliver from purgatory those who have been devoted to the Rosary.

X. The faithful children of the Rosary shall merit a high degree of glory in heaven.

XI. You shall obtain all you ask of me by the recitation of the Rosary.

XII. All those who propagate the holy Rosary shall be aided by me in their necessities.

XIII. I have obtained from my Divine Son that all the advocates of the Rosary shall have for intercessors the entire celestial court during their life and at the hour of death.

XIV. All who recite the Rosary are my sons, and brothers of my only son Jesus Christ.

XV. Devotion of my Rosary is a great sign of predestination.

(Given to St. Dominic and Blessed Alan)
Imprimatur: Patrick J. Hayes DD Archbishop of New York.

In the view of the Archdiocese of New York sometime in the tenure of Cardinal Hayes it was judged that the promises are not *contradicted* by (1) the dogmas of the Church or (2) the common Catholic doctrine of the councils and documents of the Holy See or (3) the prescriptions and thinking of approved doctors.
http://www.ncregister.com/blog/jimmy-akin/are-the/#ixzz41hzd6K7m

~~~

Origin of the Rosary

(The below section is extracted from St. Louis De Montfort's, *The Secret of the Rosary*, pp. 17-19.)

Since the Holy Rosary is composed, principally and in substance, of the Prayer of Christ and the Angelic Salutation, that is, the Our Father and the Hail Mary, it was without doubt the first prayer and the first devotion of the faithful and has been in use all through the centuries from the time of the Apostles and disciples down to the present.

But it was only in the year 1214, however, that Holy Mother Church received the Rosary in its present form and according to the method we use today. It was given to the Church by Saint Dominic who had received it from the Blessed Virgin as a powerful means of converting the Albigensians and other sinners.

I will tell you the story of how he received it, which is found in the very well-known book *De Dignitate Psalterii* by Blessed Alan de la Roche. Saint Dominic, seeing that the gravity of people's sins was hindering the conversion of the Albigensians, withdrew into a forest near Toulouse where he prayed unceasingly for three days and three nights. During this time he did nothing but weep and do harsh penances in order to appease the anger of Almighty God. He used his discipline so much that his body was lacerated, and finally he fell into a coma.

At this point Our Lady appeared to him, accompanied by three angels, and she said: "*Dear Dominic, do you know which weapon the Blessed Trinity wants to use to reform the world?*"

"Oh, my Lady," answered Saint Dominic, "you know far better than I do because next to your Son Jesus Christ you have always been the chief instrument of our salvation."

Then Our Lady replied:
"*I want you to know that, in this kind of warfare, the battering ram has always been the Angelic Psalter which is the foundation stone of the New Testament. Therefore if you want to reach these hardened souls and win them over to God, preach my Psalter.*"

Inspired by the Holy Ghost, instructed by the Blessed Virgin as well by his own experience, Saint Dominic preached the Holy Rosary for the rest of his life. He preached it by his example as well as by his sermons, in cities in country places, to people of high station and low, before scholars and the uneducated, to Catholics and to heretics.

The Holy Rosary which he said every day was his preparation for every sermon and his little tryst with Our Lady immediately after preaching.

♦♦♦

Chapter 12

Additional Selections on the Importance of Humility

Quotes from *Humility of Heart*, by Fr. Cajetan Mary da Bergamo, published by TAN Books:

The proof of true humility is patience (p. 79).

Humility generates confidence (p.97).

No one can sin as long as he is humble (p. 33).

Must we suppose that all the treasures of Divine Wisdom which were in Christ are to be reduced to the virtue of humility? "So it certainly is," answers St. Augustine. Humility contains all things because in this virtue is truth; therefore God must also dwell therein, since He is the Truth (p.3).

~~~

"Be thou filled with wonder and praise at the greatness and magnificence of the Creator and in his pesence humiliate thyself to the dust. Shun no difficulty or suffering in order to become meek and humble of heart. Take notice, my dearest, that this virtue of humility was the firm foundation of all the wonders, which the Most High wrought in me; and in order that thou mayest esteem this virtue so much the more, remember that of all the others, it is at the same time the most precious, the most delicate and perishable; for if thou lose it in any respect, and if thou be not humble in all things without exception, thou will not be humble in anything." Blessed Virgin Mary in *Mystical City of God, The Incarnation*, Chapter 1.14, Ven. Mary of Agreda.

In order that you may be fortified and rendered pleasing to Him who is humility itself, it does not suffice that you have a lowly opinion of yourself, thinking yourself unworthy of good but deserving evil. Rather you must be willing to be despised, loath to accept praise, and eager to accept contempt, being certain, however, that true humility and not a stubborn haughtiness be your real motive. (*The Spiritual Combat*, Dom Lorenzo Scupoli, TAN Books, p. 100.)

If we wish the world to look upon us as saints, we deserve a criminal's punishment. *(Ibid.*, p. 100).

~~~

Quotes from Fr. Peter J. Arnoudt's *The Imitation of the Sacred Heart of Jesus* (TAN Books):

If thou are truly humble, thou shalt captivate thy neighbor (p. 295).

Humility is the principle of all good things (p. 183).

Truth begets humility, which is the virtue of virtues, and charity gives it life and form (p. 183).

A humble heart, which is satisfied with holding an inferior place among men, and which, distrustful of self, has, in every difficulty, recourse to Jesus, can alone preserve an undisturbed peace (p. 263).

Humility is the first of virtues; no virtue is acquired without it. Humility produces all other virtues, nourishes them when produced, and preserves them safe and sound (p. 188).

It is the virtue that inspires courage – disposes the soul for the greatest deeds. For the humble man, overlooking himself, and relying upon God, exchanges his own strength, and puts on the strength of God, upon whom he rests, and in whom he can do all things (p. 189).

"Come to me, all you that labour, and are burdened, and I will refresh you. Take up my yoke upon you, and learn of me, because I am meek, and humble of heart: and you shall find rest to your souls. For my yoke is sweet and my burden light." (Mt. 11: 28-30.)

The yoke is Your Holy Will, O Lord. Our own will is burdensome and hard, and there is no rest therein.

I would learn from You O Lord for I believe in your promise, that my soul shall find rest.

I shall not fear coming to you, for you are meek and gentle.

I shall not despair of the infinite distance between us, for You shall reach down your Holy Hand. In Your humility You will not think it beneath Yourself to touch me at my own level.

You emptied yourself for us, so we must empty ourselves for You. You emptied Yourself of Your seat at the Right Hand of the Father – of Your Divinity in Its glory – to become man, one of us. So we must empty ourselves of our pride, and remove ourselves from that seat that Satan tempted us to take, when we thought we should be as gods, knowing good and evil.

The beginning of Fr. Peter J. Arnoudt's *The Imitation of the Sacred Heart of Jesus:*

The Foundation.

The voice of Jesus – Learn of Me because I am meek and humble of Heart; and ye shall find rest for your souls.

The voice of the disciple – These are the words of Jesus Christ, whereby we are commanded to learn and imitate the Virtues of His Heart, that we may be set free from all misery of soul, and be made truly happy.

This is His doctrine, this is the method of learning, this is the fruit, this is the end.

~~~

Selections from *The Practice of Humility*, by Joachim Cardinal Pecci, Bishop of Perugia, the future Pope Leo XIII:

"It is an undisputed truth that no mercy will be reserved to the proud, that the gates of heaven will be closed to them and opened only to the *humble*. To become convinced of this, it is enough to open holy Scripture, which in various places teaches: that God resists the proud and humbles the mighty; that only those who know how to become like little children will enter his glory, while those who do not bear such a resemblance will be excluded; finally that God does not bestow his grace except upon the humble. "

"Refer to God all the good you do; know that if you keep a good work hidden and secret so that only God knows it, it will reap a priceless profit. On the contrary, if by your negligence it will become known by men, it will lose almost all its value, as does a good fruit which the birds have started to eat."

"Do not flatter yourself to be able to acquire humility without those particular practices proper to it, that is, acts of meekness, patience, obedience, mortification, self-hatred, renunciation of your feelings and opinions, sorrow for your sins, and so forth. These alone, in fact, are the weapons capable of destroying in you the kingdom of self-love, that infected ground on which all vices sprout, and where your pride and presumption take root and thrive."

~~~

And finally, the words of the Blessed Mother herself, in her beautiful Magnificat prayer (Luke 1: 46-55):

And Mary said: My soul doth magnify the Lord. And my spirit hath rejoiced in God my Saviour. Because he hath regarded the humility of his handmaid; for behold from henceforth all generations shall call me blessed. Because he that is mighty, hath done great things to me; and holy is his name. And his mercy is from generation unto generations, to them that fear him.

He hath shewed might in his arm: he hath scattered the proud in the conceit of their heart. He hath put down the mighty from their seat, and hath exalted the humble. He hath filled the hungry with good things; and the rich he hath sent empty away. He hath received Israel his servant, being mindful of his mercy: As he spoke to our fathers, to Abraham and to his seed for ever.

♦♦♦

Chapter 13

Fatima and the Rosary

The apparitions – a brief sketch. In 1917 the Blessed Virgin Mary appeared on the 13th of the month to three children near Fatima, Portugal, from May to October of that year. The tree shepherd children were Francisco Marto, his sister Jacinta Marto, and their cousin Lucy dos Santos. Fancisco and Jacinta have both been declared "Blessed" by the Church, which has declared the messages of Our Lady of Fatima as worthy of belief. The children also had visions of an angel calling himself the Angel of Portugal, who prepared them for the appearance of Mary, and who taught them certain prayers.

The message of Our Lady of Fatima consisted of requests to prayer, penance, reparation, and devotion to her Immaculate Heart, the Rosary, and the Scapular. Our Lady prophesied the outbreak of the Second World War, and asked for prayers for the conversion of Russia and her consecration by the Church. The children experienced a horrifying vision of hell, but she promised that in the end her Immaculate Heart would triumph.

At her appearance on October 13, she fulfilled her promise of a miracle. The famous "miracle of the sun" was witnessed by 70,000 people, who saw a vision of the sun spin and dance in the air.

How to Pray the Secret Rosary

Besides a call to penance, Fatima is in a special way a call for the Rosary. So central is the Rosary to the Fatima message that Our Lady chose to identify herself as *"The Lady of the Rosary."* In each of the six apparitions she asked for the daily Rosary, and especially as an instrument of world peace.

> *May 13, 1917:* Say the Rosary every day to obtain world peace and the end of the war.
> *June 13, 1917:* I want you to say the Rosary every day.
> *July 13, 1917:* I want you to continue saying the Rosary every day.
> *August 19, 1917:* I want you to continue saying the Rosary every day.
> *September 13, 1917:* Continue saying the Rosary to obtain the end of the war.
> *October 13, 1917:* I want you to continue saying the Rosary every day.

As she revealed in the third apparition: *"You must recite the Rosary every day in honor of Our Lady of the Rosary to obtain peace for the world and the end of the war, for only she can obtain this."* In this Our Lady renewed her request for the prayer she gave to the Church centuries before, a prayer that has proven a powerful weapon against the enemies of Christianity as history testifies.

When asked about the importance of the Rosary, visionary Sister Lucy responded: *"My impression is*

How to Pray the Secret Rosary

that the Rosary is of greatest value not only according to the words of Our Lady at Fatima, but according to the effects of the Rosary one sees throughout history. My impression is that Our Lady wanted to give ordinary people, who might not know how to pray, this simple method of getting closer to God."

The Rosary is basically a gospel prayer, and for those who pray it properly, it is, as Sister Lucy said, *"a simple method of getting closer to God."*

The above section is taken from the web sites: http://www.Rosary-center.org/fatimams.htm#prayer and http://fatima.ageofmary.com/Rosary/

~ ~ ~

Fatima visionary Sister Lucy said in a 1957 interview given to Fr. Augustin Fuentes, that "God is giving two last remedies to the world: the Holy Rosary and devotion to the Immaculate Heart of Mary. And, being the last remedies, that is to say, they are the final ones, means that there will be no others."

In the same interview, Sister Lucy added: "Prayer and sacrifice are the two means to save the world. As for the Holy Rosary, Father, in these last times in which we are living, the Blessed Virgin has given a new efficacy to the praying of the Holy Rosary. This in such a way that there is no problem that cannot be resolved by praying the Rosary, no matter how difficult it is - be it temporal or above all spiritual - in the spiritual life of each of us or the lives of our families, be they our families in the world or Religious Communities, or even in the lives of peoples and nations.

"I repeat, there is no problem, as difficult as it may be, that we cannot resolve at this time by praying the Holy Rosary. With the Holy Rosary we will save ourselves, sanctify ourselves, console Our Lord and obtain the salvation of many souls.

"Then, there is devotion to the Immaculate Heart of Mary, our Most Holy Mother, holding her as the seat of mercy, goodness and pardon and the sure door to enter Heaven."

The above section is from the website of: http://www.traditioninaction.org/HotTopics/g23ht_Interview.html

The "Fatima" prayer.

During the third Fatima apparition on July 13, 1917 Our Lady specifically requested that what is now generally known as "The Fatima Prayer" be prayed at the end of each decade of the Rosary.

"Do you want to learn a prayer?" the vision asked, "Yes we do!" the children responded. "When you recite the Rosary, say at the end of each decade: Oh My Jesus, forgive us our sins, save us from the fires of hell, and lead all souls to Heaven, especially those in most need of Your Mercy."

http://www.theholyrosary.org/fatimaapparitions

♦♦♦

Chapter 14

Padre Pio and the Rosary

St. Padre Pio famously called the Rosary his "weapon." He prayed an incredible number of rosaries a day, and offered his life to avert a universal cataclysm.

St. Pio's Superior at the Friary, Padre Carmelo, recalled that one night, with two other Friars, he entered the cell of his spiritual father in order to wish him good night. They found him ready for bed, with a little cap on his head, tied with two loops around his neck, and with white half-gloves covering his wounded hands. To his visitors he explained: "I must pray two and a half rosaries before going to sleep". And in response to the question of Padre Carmelo as to how many he had said during the day he replied: "To my Superior I must tell the truth: I have said thirty-four. I am able to recite so many because when I hear confessions and the penitents are going to need time, first I make them tell their sins, and then I permit them to speak about any others they might have. And while listening to them I say the Rosary. But this, thirty-six in one day, is not for you. It is enough for you to pray fewer, but it is necessary to pray, to pray."

Padre Carmelo was eventually transferred, but during the last years of Padre Pio's life, often visited him.

The cruel reality, that of a man very ill and morally crushed, was evident during these visits from Padre Pio's ex-Superior. Upon this holy Friar, Padre Carmelo recounted, was imposed the obedience of praying of only one Rosary per day, according to the Conventual rules, an absurd chastisement, very painful for one who normally prayed thirty-six daily, passing the night in prayer. Moreover, he was forced to limit his confessions, to rest more, and to eat more; the pretense being for his physical well-being. But they never took into account the transcendental dimensions into which he had soared in the last years of his life, thereby indirectly putting into doubt his very sanctity.

Padre Carmelo: "In my memory my spiritual Father is similar to the figures of the Old Testament at the end of their days, a new Moses, leading not only one group of people, but a whole multitude of peoples disseminated throughout the globe. I kneeled before him to kiss his hand and to give him a filial embrace. He returned the embrace and smiled without speaking. His confrere Padre Mariano asked him "Do you recognize who this is?" The holy Friar looked at him with a stare as if he were coming out from a state of ecstasy with the Lord, and spoke: "Yes, I recognize him." Then he said this, word for word: "My son, I offer my life to the Lord *in order to avert a universal cataclysm"*.

How to Pray the Secret Rosary

The above section was translated by Frank Rega from "The Gospel of Padre Pio" a series of three articles running once a week in the Italian magazine *Oggi*, based on interviews with Padre Carmelo, who when young was the spiritual child of Padre Pio, and later in life became his Superior at the Friary in San Giovanni Rotondo. The articles were published beginning April 28, 1999, and were written by Gisella Pagano and Matilde Amorosi.

~ ~ ~

Some of Padre Pio's spiritual children posed the following to Padre Pio:

When I recite the Rosary, Father, should I pay more attention to the Hail Marys or to the mystery? Padre Pio's answer: To the Hail Marys of the mystery you are contemplating.

Intercede for me, Father, to get the punishment for my sins lightened. Answer: Enrich yourself with indulgences. Recite the Rosary in front of Jesus in the Most Holy Sacrament of the Altar.

How many Rosaries should I recite, Father? Answer: When I've recited the Rosary 180 times, I rest.
How do you manage to recite so many? Answer: As you manage not to.
Do you recite them at night, too? Answer: Obviously.

How to Pray the Secret Rosary

Above section taken from *Padre Pio Teaches Us*, pp. 199-200.

~ ~ ~

"Our Lady of Fatima asked especially for the prayer of the Rosary. And who could count the hours Padre Pio spent in prayer for the conversion and salvation of sinners? And who more than he held the Rosary in his hand, night and day, filling all the free moments of the day with the most devout recital of the Rosary? And with how much loving insistence did he not recommend the Rosary to everyone as a means of salvation!

"One day one of his penitents said to him: "Padre, today they say the Rosary is out of date, that it is no longer in fashion. It is no longer said in many churches." He replied: "Let us do what our fathers did and all will be well with us." "But Satan rules the world." Padre Pio replied: "Because they make him rule; can a spirit rule by itself if it is not united to the human will? We could not have been born in a more depraved world. The one who prays a lot saves himself. The one who prays little is in danger. The one who does not pray loses his soul."

"Padre, say something to us."

"Love our Lady, make others love her. Always say your Rosary and say it well. Satan always tries to destroy this prayer, but he will never succeed. It is the prayer of her who triumphs over everything and everyone."

And two days before he died, he repeated: "Love our Lady and make her loved. Recite the Rosary and recite it always. And recite it as much as you can."

The above section is taken from an article written by Most Rev. Paola Carta, Bishop Emeritus of Foggia, "Padre Pio and the Immaculate Heart of Mary," published in the *Voice of Padre Pio* magazine, July 1997, and made available many web sites including: http://www.ewtn.com/padrepio/mystic/Mary.htm.

~ ~ ~

"As one would expect from someone so filled with the love of Mary and so convinced of the power of the Rosary, Padre Pio recommended both to all who approached him and particularly to his "spiritual children" who sought his very special protection and help. He sent them all to the mother of Jesus and told them to say the Rosary every day.

"Padre Pio's example confirmed his words. He gave the example of private, personal use of the Rosary, as well as public recitation of that prayer. Those who saw Padre Pio in what he called his free moments, as he walked from one place to another, will remember him holding the Rosary to his breast and praying it as he walked. Father Eusebio of Castelpetroso, a Capuchin who was Padre Pio's constant companion for five years, once decoyed him into revealing that on a particular day he had said 60 rosaries of 15 decades. It must be remembered that Padre Pio slept at the most two or three hours a night, never continuously, and often he never slept at all. The precise number of rosaries he said each day, of course, is not the point. The point is that he prayed the Rosary continually in his free moments."

The above section is taken from "Padre Pio, Mary, and the Rosary," an article written by Fr. Joseph A. Pelletier, which is made available on many online web sites such as http://www.garabandal.us/padre_maryrosary.

~ ~ ~

The following are some selected remarks by Padre Pio on the Rosary compiled by Guiseppe Caccioppoli at http://caccioppoli.com/index.htm, used with permisison.

To father Onorato Marcucci, grabbing the Rosary that he had put few seconds beforehand on the nightstand: "With this, one wins the battles."

Father Marcellino testified that he had to help Padre Pio wash his hands one at a time "because he didn't want to leave the Rosary beads, and passed the Rosary from one hand to the other."

About the repetitiveness of the Rosary: "Pay attention to the mysteries. They change at every decade."

How to Pray the Secret Rosary

To Enedina Mori: "When you get tired reciting the Rosary, rest a bit, and then restart again."

"The Rosary is the weapon given us by Mary to use against the tricks of the infernal enemy."

"Mary has taught us the Rosary just as Jesus taught us the Our Father".

◆◆◆

How to Pray the Secret Rosary

How to Pray the Secret Rosary

Chapter 15

How many Rosaries Should One Pray?

Catholic author Mary O'Regan writes for England's *Catholic Herald* and is also an editor (John Carmichael's *Drunks and Monks*). The selection below is from her influential blog "The Path Less Taken."
http://thepathlesstaken7.blogspot.com/2014/06/padre-pio-on-Rosary.html.

~ ~ ~

"Padre Pio said the Rosary as often as was humanly possible for him, and on one occasion when he was asked to pray more, he said that it was impossible for him to do so, because he was already praying the Rosary at every spare moment. My one reservation would be that I've known quite a number of people, especially mothers who are worried about the state of the world, and who become unhealthily obsessive about the Rosary for a short time. They say four to eight Rosaries a day, while neglecting other duties such as eating regularly, caring for their kids or attending to their job. It catches up with them, they might get fired or sick, and then they react negatively by dropping the Rosary altogether, so they go from saying it many times a day to not saying it at all.

"It's good to be balanced and do as Our Lady asked and say one five decade Rosary each and every day, while saying more Rosaries if we have the occasion. It may seem 'weaker' and 'less committed' than the fired-up person who says four Rosaries a day for a short period of time and then burns out. But do the sums. If someone says four Rosaries a day for two months and then stops for good, they will have said about 240 Rosaries for that year. But if someone commits to saying a five decade Rosary each day, and recites it every day for a year, they will have said 365 in one year.

"If the Rosary is our weapon or our defence, then the person who says it everyday is like the person who locks their house at night, keeps their valuables in a safe and has a pepper spray in their pocket in case they are attacked in public. While the person who goes through a phase of saying it eight times a day, is like someone who temporarily makes their home like a maximum security prison, only to suddenly stop saying it, thus making their home like a building with broken windows and doors hanging off their hinges."

♦♦♦

Bibliography

Scripture Quotations generally are from the Douay Rheims version of *The Holy Bible*, Rockford Il., TAN Books and Publishers, 1971. Also online at http://www.drbo.org/index.htm.

~ ~ ~

Agreda, Ven. Mary of, *Mystical City of God, the Incarnation*, Washington, N.J., Ave Maria Institute, 1971.

Anonymous, *The Cloud of Unknowing*, W. Johnston, editor, Image Books, U.S., 1973.

Arnoudt, Rev. Peter J., *The Imitation of the Sacred Heart of Jesus*, Rockford, Il., TAN Books and Publishers, 1974.

Aquinas, St. Thomas, *Summa Theologica*, New York, Benziger Brothers, Inc., 1947, 3 Volumes.

Aquinas, St. Thomas, works are online at
http://dhspriory.org/thomas/

Augustine, St., *The Lord's Sermon on the Mount,* New York, Newman Press, 1948.

Augustine, St., *The Trinity*, Washington D.C., Catholic University of America Press, 1963.

Augustine, St., works are online at www.newadvent.org/fathers/

Bergamo, Fr. Cajetan Mary da, *Humilty of Heart*, Rockford, Il., TAN Books and Publishers, 1978.

Caussade, Jean-Pierre de, *Abandonment to Divine Providence,* Image Classics, 1993.

Cushing, Cardinal Richard, *Eternal Thoughts of Christ the Teacher, Vol. 2,* Boston, St. Paul Editions, 1961.

Drexelius, Fr. Jeremias, *The Heliotropium*, Rockford Il., TAN Books and Publishers, Inc., 1984.

Eymard, St. Peter Julian, *The Real Presence*, New York, Eymard League, 1938.

Julian of Norwich, *Revelations of Divine Love*, Brewster, Ma., Paraclete Press, 2011.

Liguori, St. Aphonsus, *The Glories of Mary,* Rockford Il., TAN Books and Publishers, 1977.

Liguori, St. Aphonsus, *The Holy Eucharist,* Brooklyn, Redemptorist Fathers, 1934.

Liguori, St. Aphonsus, *The Incarnation, Birth and Infancy of Jesus Christ,* Brooklyn, Redemptorist Fathers, 1927.

Montfort, St. Louis De, *The Secret of the Rosary*, Rockford Il, TAN Books and Publishers, 1965.

Padre Pio, *Counsels,* Fr. Alessio Parente, Editor, San Giovanni Rotondo, It., Our Lady of Grace Friary, 1984.

Padre Pio, *Padre Pio Teaches Us*, Rev. Nello Castello, Editor, San Giovanni Rotondo, It., La Casa Sollievo della Sofferenza Editions, 1981.

Palau, Fr. Gabriel S.J., *The Active Catholic*, Rockford Il., TAN Books and Publishers, 2001.

Pallen, Conde B., editor, *The New Catholic Dictionary*, New York, Universal Knowledge Foundatin, 1929.

Piccarreta, Luisa, *The Book of Heaven*, Frank Albas, Editor, Miami Beach, Fla. https://www.divinewill.cc/

Pecci, Joachim Cardinal [the future Pope Leo XIII], *The Practice of Humility*, Boston, Daughters of St. Paul, 1978.

Scupoli, Dom Lorenzo, *The Spiritual Combat*, Rockford, Il.,TAN Books and Publishers, 1990.

Sheen, Bishop Fulton J., *The Cross and the Beatitudes*, Liguori, Mo, Liguori/Triumph, 2000.

Saint-Laurent, Thomas de, *Confidence*, Dublin, Browne and Nolan Ltd., 1932.

Trent, Council of, *The Catechism of the Council of Trent*, Rockford, Il., TAN Books and Publishers, 1982.

♦♦♦

About the Author

The author, Frank M. Rega OSF is a Third Order Franciscan and the author of many books and articles on Catholic saints and mystics, including St. Padre Pio, St. Francis of Assisi, and Luisa Piccarreta. His gateway web page is www.frankrega.com and his email address is regaf@aya.yale.edu.

Made in the USA
Monee, IL
08 February 2021